FOR OUR ARMED FORCES

Compiled by
Paul Pennick and
Joseph Nonnenkamp

Liguori
ONE LIGUORI DRIVE
LIGUORI MO 63057-9999

Imprimi Potest:
Thomas D. Picton, C.Ss.R.
Provincial, Denver Province
The Redemptorists

© 2005, Liguori Publications
ISBN 0-7648-1311-0
Printed in the United States of America
05 06 07 08 09 5 4 3 2 1

Liguori Publications, a nonprofit corporation, is an
apostolate of the Redemptorists. To learn more about the
Redemptorists, visit Redemptorists.com.

Select prayers taken from Jennifer Martinez online
(www.jenmartinez.com).

Short Prayers for the Long Day, compiled by Giles and Helville
Harcourt, © 1978, Published by Liguori Publications 1996.

The People's Prayer Book, edited by Carole Garibaldi Rogers
and Mary Ann Jeselson, © 2003, Published by Liguori Publications.

To order call 1-800-325-9521
www.liguori.org

FOREWORD

Several years ago in Chicago I was standing outside St. Michael's Church. Suddenly, the church door opened. Out stepped an 8-year-old girl. I asked her, "Where have you been?"

Pointing to the church, she answered "in there."

Then I questioned her, "What were you doing in there?"

Her response was, "I was praying."

Thinking the youngster might have some problem at home or in school, I prodded her, "What were you praying for?"

"Nothing" was her reply. "I was just loving God."

That response of the youngster evokes a refreshing note in our lives, especially against the background statistics of certain religious surveys. Many church leaders sound alarmed when so-called experts inform them that only 40 percent of Americans attend worship services once a week. Perhaps a more hopeful picture of people's relationship to God surfaces from a sociologist-priest, Father Andrew Greeley. According to his studies at a research center, quoted by *Newsweek* magazine from the early 1990s, 78 percent of all Americans pray at least once a week, more than 57 percent report praying once a day. Strangely enough, among the 13 percent of Americans who claim to be atheists, one in five still prays daily.

Personally, I believe, Liguori's new booklet on prayer, specifically for those in the military and their families seems timely. Prayer often seems a result, or even a refuge from certain danger. In fact, during the Second World War, the common expression "there are no atheists in fox holes" underlined people's turning to God as a final, desperate clutching effort.

However, I believe that in some, even sneaky way, God has buried deep in every human heart a need that Saint Augustine explains so well, "our hearts are restless, Lord, until they rest in you." Prayer becomes a better measuring rod of our relationship to God than perhaps attendance at church.

In our efforts at Liguori to provide a handy spiritual weapon with this practical booklet for military personnel and their families, we also take this opportunity to praise these dedicated heroes for casting aside their own selfish needs to provide freedom for all of us in this country we lovingly treasure.

FATHER JAMES T. GLEASON, C.SS.R.
AIR FORCE CHAPLAIN 1958-1963

KEEP THEM IN YOUR CARE

Almighty God, we commend to your gracious care and keeping all the men and women of our armed forces at home and abroad. Defend them day by day with your heavenly grace; strengthen them in their trials and temptations; give them courage to face the perils which beset them; and grant them a sense of your abiding presence wherever they may be; through Jesus Christ our Lord.

Amen.

IN YOUR HANDS

Lord, hold our troops in your loving hands. Protect them as they protect us. Bless them and their families for the selfless acts they perform for us in our time of need. I ask this in the name of Jesus, our Lord and Savior.

Amen.

✠

GUIDANCE AND PROTECTION

I asked the Lord to bless you
As I pray for you today
To guide you and protect you
As you go along your way.

His love is always with you
His promises are true
And when we give him all our cares
You know he will see you through.

So when the road you're traveling on
Seems difficult at best
Just remember I'm praying
And God will do the rest.

Amen.

B.J. MORBITZER

✠

Psalm of Praise in Time of Sorrow and Fear

(Based on Psalm 146: Constant Is God's Love)

Praise God! Praise the God who created all
things, O my soul!
I will praise God as long as I live
   I will sing praises to my God all
   my life long.

Do not put your trust in human help.
   When their breath departs, they return
   to the soil;
   on that very day their plans perish
   with them.

Happy are those whose help is from God,
whose hope is in their God,
who made heaven and earth, the sea, and all
that is in them; who keeps faith forever;
   who executes justice for the oppressed;
   who gives food to the hungry.

Only God sets the prisoners free;
   Only God opens the eyes of the blind.
   God lifts up those who are bowed down
   and loves the righteous.
   God watches over strangers;
   God upholds the orphan, widow, and
   soldier, but brings to ruin the way of the
   wicked.
Praise God who will reign forever, your God,
Creator and Lover of us all, for all
generations.
Praise God, O, my soul! Praise God!
                    Amen.
                    DEBBIE MEISTER

✠

PSALM OF LAMENTATION
FOR THE WOUNDED

O, God, in your great mercy,
receive the prayers of the wounded.
Do you hear their voices
as they cry out
with fear
and in pain?
Their eyes do not see you,
in the darkness
falling around them.

Bravely have they fought,
with honor have they fallen.
Lift them, God of strength and healing,
from the blood soaked ground.

The earth moans with their pain,
ready to claim them.
Rescue them, God of Light,
and carry them to safety.

O, God, whose Word gives comfort,
speak now into their hearts.
Will they hear your voice
in the chaos
of terror
and anguish?
They remember your promise,
to protect those
fighting for justice.

In you, O God, they trust,
with undying hope
they wait.
Bring them safely home.
Amen.
DEBBIE MEISTER

Psalm of Lamentation with All Who Suffer Disabilities From War

Creator God, living and eternal,
O Holy One of power,
You created out of darkness all life
and shaped us in your image.
Where is the power of your love now?

God of mercy, healing, and hope,
You are silent and we cannot hear you.
We are deaf to your Word,
blind to the path that will take us home,
powerless to move on our own.

You have made us in your image
But we are flawed.
Unable, disabled, all of us,
each in our own way
helpless, weak, and afraid.
We are broken and in pain.
We pray for healing,

Day after day,
but today is like yesterday
and we remain unchanged.

Like the blind, and lame, and deaf
who came to Jesus
begging for mercy
We cry and weep for one another
and for ourselves.

We feel alone, searching for the love
you have promised to give us
in our faithfulness.
But find only silence,
except for our own voices
crying out to you for mercy.

Our woundedness is real
to us, more real than your presence.
We weep for ourselves,
hopeless, O God, we cry out to you
and ask you to heal our brokenness.

You have shaped us, God,
most loving creator,
into the Body of Christ.
Yet, in our brokenness we see
as separate souls,
and we do not always recognize
the suffering of the one beside us.

Love us, God of eternal promise,
into life.
Lead us, by the light of your Son,
to new life.
We long for wholeness in you,
Living God.

Amen.

DEBBIE MEISTER

PRAYER FOR ABSENT FAMILY MEMBERS

O God, whose fatherly care reaches to the uttermost parts of the earth; We humbly beseech you graciously to behold and bless those whom we love, now absent from us. Defend them from all dangers of soul and body, and grant that both they and we, drawing nearer to you, may be bound together by your love in the communion of your Holy Spirit; through Jesus Christ our Lord.

Amen.

✠

In Times of Weariness

Jesus, my shepherd,
sometimes the excitement of my ministry
is matched only by the fatigue
that creeps in upon me.
When I grow weary
help me to have the wisdom to stop,
even if briefly,
to sit a while with you and listen to you.
In my rest, open my eyes anew
to the many around me who need a touch,
a word, or a companion,
and grant me the grace to respond
with generous compassion
as I have seen you do.

Amen.

✠

Prayer for Our Protectors

Our Father, in these hours of daylight we remember those who must wake that we may sleep; bless those who watch over us at night, the guardians of the peace, the watchers who save us from the terror of fire, and all the many who carry on through the hours of the night, the restless commerce of men on land and sea. We thank thee for their faithfulness and sense of duty; we pray thee for thy pardon if our covetousness or luxury make their nightly toil necessary; grant that we may realize how dependent the safety of our loved ones and the comforts of life are on these our brothers, that so we may think of them with love and gratitude and help to make their burden lighter. Through Jesus Christ our Lord.

Amen.

PEACE

Peace is so hard to build
so easy to destroy.
Peace of mind
Peace of heart
Peace of home
Peace of land.
We thank you Lord this day
for all those who have given their
lives in war
that we might live in peace,
and, in gratitude, become in turn
living instruments of peace:
Peace in mind
Peace in heart
Peace in home
Peace in land.

Amen.

GILES HARCOURT

✠

MORNING PRAYER

Grant, O Lord,

that we may approach every question of foreign policy from the point of sight in our creed; that we may check in ourselves and in others every temper which makes for war, all ungenerous judgements, all presumptuous claims, all promptings of self-assertion, the growth of ignorance and passion;

that we may endeavor to understand the needs, the feelings, the endowments, the traditional aspirations of other countries;

that we may do gladly, unweariedly, patiently, what lies in us to remove suspicions and misunderstandings; that we may honor all men.

Amen.

BISHOP WESTCOTT, 1825-1901

✠
FOR THE SUFFERING

Mary, Mother of Sorrows
and Comforter of the Afflicted.
grant that we may share with you
in the pain of your Son's sufferings.
As you were so fully present
to the agony of your Son,
may we too be present to the pain
and suffering of those in our midst
and, through our compassion and love,
bring to them a measure of consolation,
through the same Christ our Lord.
Amen.

✠

GREY DAYS

God of our life there are days when the burdens we carry chafe our shoulders and weigh us down; when the road seems dreary and endless, the skies grey and threatening; when our lives have no music in them, and our hearts are lonely, and our souls have lost their courage. Flood the path with light, we beseech you, tune our hearts to brave music; give us the sense of comradeship with heroes and saints of every age; and so quicken our spirits that we may be able to encourage the souls of all who journey with us on the road of life, to your honor and glory.

Amen.

✠

PRAYER FROM SAINT IGNATIUS

O Lord Jesus Christ,
take as your right,
receive as my gift,
all my liberty,
my memory,
my understanding,
my will,
all that I have
all that I am
all that I can be.
To you, O Lord, I restore it,
all is yours,
dispose of it according to your will.
Give me your love.
Give me your grace.
It is enough for me.

Amen.

PRAYER FOR STORMY TIMES

Creator of the wind and sea,
storms and distractions abound
as we move through our daily lives.
When all around us is crashing and
shifting,
we often lose our ability
to keep our eyes and hearts trained on you.
We forget who you are
and our faith becomes fragile.
During these times, bring to mind
the many ways you have been present to us
in the past,
and help us to experience your presence.
Forgive us when we doubt you,
and deepen our ability to trust.
I offer this prayer through Christ our Lord.
Amen.

✠

Prayer for the Injured

Breathe down, O Lord, upon all those who are bearing pain, thy spirit of healing, thy spirit of life, thy spirit of peace and hope, of love and joy, thy spirit of courage and endurance. Cast out from them the spirit of anxiety and fear, grant them perfect confidence and trust in thee, that in thy light they may see light.

Amen.

DIANA PONSONBY

☩

A New World

We pray, Father of all, who loves all men, for a new Britain, a new Europe, a new America, a new Asia, and a new world, wherein every race may be free, and government may be of the people, by all and for all, so that the nations, ordering their states wisely and worthily, may live in the example of your Son Jesus Christ our Lord, to whom with the Father and the Holy Spirit, may all the praise of the world be given, all power, dominion and glory for ever.

Amen.

For Courage to Serve

God of our hopes and our dreams,
you have planted the hunger
for glad tidings within us.
Make your joy more complete
as we participate in proclaiming
this Good News;
the blind will see, the prisoner will be released.
Give us the courage to reach out to the
incarcerated and bring into reality
this promise of freedom.
Help us to diffuse our fears
and know how to realize our calls so that a
year of favor may be celebrated in your name.
I pray this,
holding my reservations and anxiety up to you,
and I ask for your blessing and grace,
through Jesus Christ, our Lord
and through your Holy Spirit.

Amen.

✠

THE PRESENCE OF GOD

Heavenly Father, you created
all peoples of every nation
in your image and likeness.
Open our eyes
to the strength of your love for all people.
Open our minds
to your intervention
in every pressing human situation
and social issue.
Give us the humility and discernment
to enter into your love, mercy, justice,
and patience
for all humanity.
Open our hearts
to your compassionate understanding.
Show us where to begin.
We ask this through your Son, Jesus,
our Lord and brother.

Amen.

☩

IN TIMES OF STRUGGLE

Jesus,
how often I find myself like Peter—
quick to call you Lord and Savior,
but slow to embrace your sacrificial
and saving way.
I confess I am more comfortable
with your resurrection than with
your passion.
Thank you, Jesus,
for your example of sacrificial love.
Thank you for your loving assurance
that my yoke will, indeed,
be easy and my burden light.
Help me to see my daily struggles
as opportunities to follow you
by embracing my cross and
drinking my cup
as wholeheartedly as you did.

Help me to find sisters and brothers
willing to embrace
this sacrificial calling with me.
And whenever I cry out in my pain
for mercy,
please send me the same
consoling Spirit
who consoled you
in your moment of agony
in the Garden of Gethsemane.
I pray in your name, Jesus,
to our heavenly Father,
with whom you live and reign,
in the unity of the Holy Spirit,
one God,
forever and ever.

Amen.

✠

In Times of Loss

Our Father, we are gathered here
as grieving people,
as people who are lost.
We are looking for your dwelling place.
We pray that you will send your Spirit
to accompany us on this journey,
so that we are able to see hope.
In our time of loss or trouble,
help us discover new rituals for our lives.
Guide us as you will, so that we
may have new life in you.
We ask this in Jesus' name
and in the power of the Holy Spirit.
                    Amen.

✠

PRAYER FOR THE US NAVY

O eternal Lord, God, you alone spread out the heavens and rule the raging sea. Take into your most gracious protection our country's navy and all who serve therein. Preserve them from the dangers of the sea and from the violence of the enemy, that they may be a safeguard unto the United States of America, and a security for such as sail upon the seas in peaceful and lawful missions. In serving you, O Lord, may our Sailors serve their country; through Jesus Christ, our Lord.

Amen.

✝

A Soldier's Prayer

Lord Jesus, Mighty Warrior and Prince of Peace, all glory and power is yours, I offer myself and my military career for the welfare of our nation and for your glory.

You said "Blessed is the nation whose God is the Lord"; make us mindful of our nation's heritage and of who we are. You said, "Be strong and of good courage," this is my prayer. You said, "A King is not saved by his great army; a warrior is not delivered by his great strength"; be my protection and my strength. While I defend the nation, may all of heaven safeguard my family back home.

Almighty God, when you will to safely return me home, help me to see in each member of my family all that I am willing to fight for— life, liberty, freedom, and justice. Give me wisdom to share what experiences would lead my sons to Christ—like valor, my daughters to Christian compassion. When Mary witnessed you falling wounded to the ground, she reaffirmed her trust in God her savior. Fill my spouse with surety in your divine plan for me, our family and our nation. You called me to be a soldier, march along side me. Jesus, I place my trust in you.

Amen.

✠

THE MARINE PRAYER

Almighty Father, whose command is over all and whose love never fails, make me aware of thy presence and obedient to thy will. Keep me true to my best self, guarding me against dishonesty in purpose and deed and helping me to live so that I can face my fellow Marines, my loved ones, and thee without shame or fear. Protect my family.

Give me the will to do the work of a Marine and to accept my share of responsibilities with vigor and enthusiasm. Grant me the courage to be proficient in my daily performance. Keep me loyal and faithful to my superiors and to the duties my country and the Marine Corps have entrusted to me. Help me to wear my uniform with dignity, and let it remind me daily of the traditions which I must uphold.

If I am inclined to doubt, steady my faith; if I am tempted, make me strong to resist; if I should miss the mark, give me courage to try again. Guide me with the light of truth and grant me wisdom by which I may understand the answer to my prayer. *Semper Fidelis.*

Amen.

✠ AIR FORCE HYMN

Lord, guard and guide the ones who fly.
Through the great spaces of the sky
Be with them traversing the air
In darkening storms or sunshine fair.

You who keep with tender might
The balanced birds in all their flight
Lord of the tempered winds, be near
That, having you, they know no fear.

Control their minds with instinct fit
Whenever adventuring they quit
Firm security of land
Grand steadfast eye and skillful hand.

Aloft in solitudes of space.
Uphold them with your saving grace
Oh God, protect the ones who fly
Through lonely ways beneath the sky.
Amen.

CD HAMILTON, 1915, QUEBEC, LM HENRY BAKER, 1854

✠

Coast Guard Prayer

Almighty and everlasting God, we offer our prayers for those who serve in our Coast Guard. We are mindful of their traditions of selfless service to the seafarers.

Employ their devotions of good ends as they track the weather and search the seas for those in extremity of storm, shipwreck, or battle. Make their soundings and markings sure that safe passages may be found by those who go down to the sea in ships.

Encourage them, O Lord, as they stand guard over our coasts and the bulwarks of our freedoms. Graciously deliver them from threatening calamities in all their perilous voyages. Bless the keepers of the lights and be thou their close friend in lonely watches. Keep the beacons of honor and duty burning that they may reach the home port .

Amen.

✠

Special Forces Prayer

Almighty God who art the Author of liberty and the Champion of the oppressed hear our prayer. We the men of Special Forces acknowledge our dependence upon thee in the preservation of human freedom.

Go with us as we seek to defend the defenseless and to free the enslaved. May we ever remember that our nation, whose oath "in God We Trust," expects that we shall requite ourselves with honor, that we may never bring shame upon our faith, our families, or our fellow men.

Grant us wisdom from thy mind, courage from thine heart, and protection by thine hand. It is for thee that we do battle, and to thee belong's the victor's crown. For thine is the kingdom, and the power, and glory forever.

Amen.

✛

Combat Medic Prayer

Oh Lord, I ask for your divine strength to meet the demands of my profession. Help me to be the finest medic, both technically and tactically. If I am called to the battlefield, give me the courage to conserve our fighting forces by providing medical care to all who are in need. If I am called to a mission of peace, give me the strength to lead by caring for those who need my assistance. Finally, Lord, help me take care of my own spiritual, physical, and emotional needs. Teach me to trust in your presence and never-failing love.

Amen.

PRAYER FOR THE TROOPS IN IRAQ

Dear Lord, please hold our troops in your loving hands. Protect them, Father, as they protect us. When they are tired, give them strength and rest. If they are wounded, Father, give them comfort. When they are lonely, may they feel you near them. Grant them strength, courage, and wisdom for their tasks. And, Lord, uplift and strengthen the families and loved ones who wait for their return. Please, Father, bring a quick end to all this conflict. I pray in the name of Jesus, our Savior.

Amen.

✠

PRAYER FOR PRISONERS OF WAR

Lord, I bring before you now our soldiers who have been captured, and ask that you would uphold them with your right hand. Be their rock in the midst of uncertainty and their light in the midst of darkness. Guard their hearts from fear and strengthen them according to your word. Cause them, Lord, to lie down and sleep in peace for you alone are their safety.

Surround them, Lord, with your favor as a shield. Soften the hearts of those who watch over them and cause them to show compassion and mercy. Keep the hearts of our soldiers filled with hope, and guard them from despair. Be near to them, Lord, for your nearness is their good, and bring them back safely to their families. In Jesus' mighty name.

Amen.

✠

ASKING DIVINE PROTECTION
FOR THOSE IN SERVICE

O God, I beseech you, watch over those exposed to the horror of war, and the spiritual dangers of a soldier or sailor's life.

Give them such a strong faith that no human respect may ever lead them to deny it, nor fear ever to practice it. By your grace, O God, fortify them against the contagion of bad example, that being preserved from vice, and serving you faithfully, they may be ready to meet you face to face when they are so called, through Christ our Lord.

Amen.

✠

INSPIRE THEM

Sacred Heart! Inspire them with sorrow for sin, and grant them pardon.

Mother of God! Be with them on the battlefield during life and at the hour of death, and grant that they may live and die in the grace of they Son.

Saint Joseph! Pray for them. May their Guardian Angel protect them.

Amen.

✠

NIGHT PRAYER

Grant us, O Lord our God, ever to find in
   thee a very present help in trouble.
When we are in the darkness of doubt
   or perplexity,
shed thy light upon our way.
When we are burdened with the affairs
   of our daily life,
lift us to the calm of thy presence.
When we are battling with temptation and
   the flesh is weak,
by the light of thy Spirit make us strong
   to overcome.
We ask these things through him in whom we
   are more than conquerors,
thy Son Jesus Christ our Lord.
                    Amen.

WE BESEECH THEE

Lord, Jesus, we beseech thee, by the loneliness of thy suffering on the Cross, be nigh unto all them that are desolate and in pain or sorrow today; and let thy presence transform their loneliness into comfort, consolation, and holy fellowship with thee.

Amen.

✠
Psalm 23

The LORD is my shepherd, I shall not want.
    He makes me lie down in green pastures;
he leads me beside still waters;
    he restores my soul.
He leads me in right paths for his name's sake.

Even though I walk through the darkest valley,
    I fear no evil;
for you are with me;
    your rod and your staff—
    they comfort me.

You prepare a table before me
    in the presence of my enemies;
you anoint my head with oil;
    my cup overflows.
Surely goodness and mercy shall follow me
    all the days of my life,
and I shall dwell in the house of the LORD
    my whole life long.

✠
Psalm 27

The LORD is my light and my salvation;
  whom shall I fear?
The LORD is the stronghold of my life;
  of whom shall I be afraid?

When evildoers assail me
  to devour my flesh—
my adversaries and foes—
  they shall stumble and fall.

Though an army encamp against me,
  my heart shall not fear;
though war rise up against me,
  yet I will be confident.

One thing I asked of the LORD,
  that will I seek after:
to live in the house of the LORD
  all the days of my life,
to behold the beauty of the LORD,
  and to inquire in his temple.

For he will hide me in his shelter
in the day of trouble;
he will conceal me under the cover of his tent;
he will set me high on a rock.

Now my head is lifted up
above my enemies all around me,
and I will offer in his tent
sacrifices with shouts of joy;
I will sing and make melody to the LORD.

Hear, O LORD, when I cry aloud,
be gracious to me and answer me!
"Come," my heart says, "seek his face!"
Your face, LORD, do I seek.
Do not hide your face from me.

Do not turn your servant away in anger,
you who have been my help.
Do not cast me off, do not forsake me,
O God of my salvation!
If my father and mother forsake me,
the LORD will take me up.

Teach me your way, O LORD,
  and lead me on a level path
  because of my enemies.
Do not give me up to the will of
    my adversaries,
  for false witnesses have risen against me,
  and they are breathing out violence.

I believe that I shall see the goodness of
    the LORD
  in the land of the living.
Wait for the LORD;
  be strong, and let your heart take courage;
  wait for the LORD!

✛
Psalm 61

Hear my cry, O God;
  listen to my prayer.
From the end of the earth I call to you,
  when my heart is faint.

Lead me to the rock
  that is higher than I;
for you are my refuge,
  a strong tower against the enemy.

Let me abide in your tent forever,
  find refuge under the shelter of
    your wings.
For you, O God, have heard my vows;
  you have given me the heritage of those
    who fear your name.

Prolong the life of the king;
    may his years endure to all generations!
May he be enthroned forever before God;
    appoint steadfast love and faithfulness
        to watch over him!

So I will always sing praises to your name,
    as I pay my vows day after day.

☩ PSALM 140

Deliver me, O LORD, from evildoers;
  protect me from those who are violent,
who plan evil things in their minds
  and stir up wars continually.
They make their tongue sharp as a snake's,
  and under their lips is the venom of vipers.

Guard me, O LORD, from the hands of the
    wicked;
  protect me from the violent
  who have planned my downfall.
The arrogant have hidden a trap for me,
  and with cords they have spread a net,
  along the road they have set snares for me.

I say to the LORD, "You are my God;
  give ear, O LORD, to the voice of my
    supplications."

O LORD, my Lord, my strong deliverer,
    you have covered my head in the day
        of battle.
Do not grant, O LORD, the desires of
        the wicked;
    do not further their evil plot.

Those who surround me lift up their heads;
    let the mischief of their lips overwhelm
        them!
Let burning coals fall on them!
    Let them be flung into pits, no more
        to rise!
Do not let the slanderer be established in the
        land;
    let evil speedily hunt down the violent!

I know that the LORD maintains the cause of
        the needy,
    and executes justice for the poor.
Surely the righteous shall give thanks to your
        name;
    the upright shall live in your presence.

✠

Psalm 143

Hear my prayer, O LORD;
   give ear to my supplications in your
      faithfulness;
   answer me in your righteousness.
Do not enter into judgment with your
      servant,
   for no one living is righteous before you.

For the enemy has pursued me,
   crushing my life to the ground,
   making me sit in darkness like those long
      dead.
Therefore my spirit faints within me;
   my heart within me is appalled.

I remember the days of old,
   I think about all your deeds,
   I meditate on the works of your hands.
I stretch out my hands to you;
   my soul thirsts for you like a parched land.

Answer me quickly, O LORD;
   my spirit fails.
Do not hide your face from me,
   or I shall be like those who go down to the Pit.
Let me hear of your steadfast love in the
      morning,
   for in you I put my trust.
Teach me the way I should go,
   for to you I lift up my soul.

Save me, O LORD, from my enemies;
   I have fled to you for refuge.
Teach me to do your will,
   for you are my God.
Let your good spirit lead me
   on a level path.

For your name's sake, O LORD, preserve my life.
   In your righteousness bring me out of
      trouble.
In your steadfast love cut off my enemies,
   and destroy all my adversaries,
      for I am your servant.

Sign of the Cross

In the name of the Father,
and of the Son,
and of the Holy Spirit.
Amen.

Glory Be

Glory be to the Father, and to the Son,
and to the Holy Spirit, as it was in the
beginning,
is now,
and ever shall be;
world without end.
Amen.

✠

The Hail Mary

Hail Mary, full of grace! The Lord is with
you; blessed are you among women, and
blessed is the fruit of your womb, Jesus.
Holy Mary, Mother of God,
pray for us sinners,
now and at the hour of our death.
Amen.

The Lord's Prayer

Our Father, who art in heaven,
hallowed be thy name. Thy kingdom come,
thy will be done on earth as it is in heaven.
Give us this day our daily bread,
and forgive us our trespasses,
as we forgive those who trespass against us.
And lead us not into temptation,
but deliver us from evil.
Amen.

✛

The Apostles' Creed

I believe in God, the Father almighty,
    creator of heaven and earth.
I believe in Jesus Christ, his only Son,
      our Lord.
    He was conceived by the power of the Holy
    Spirit, and born of the Virgin Mary.
    He suffered under Pontius Pilate, was
    crucified, died, and was buried.
    He descended into hell.
    On the third day he rose again.
    He ascended into heaven, and is seated
    at the right hand of the Father
    He will come again to judge the living
    and the dead.

I believe in the Holy Spirit,
    the holy catholic Church,
    the communion of saints,
    the forgiveness of sins,
    the resurrection of the body,
    and the life everlasting.
                        Amen.

✠

HAIL, HOLY QUEEN

Hail, holy Queen, Mother of Mercy! Our life, our sweetness, and our hope! To thee do we cry, poor banished children of Eve, to thee do we send up our sighs, mourning and weeping in this valley of tears. Turn, then, most gracious advocate, thine eyes of mercy toward us; and after this our exile show unto us the blessed fruit of thy womb Jesus; O clement, O loving, O sweet virgin Mary. Pray for us, O holy Mother of God, that we may be made worthy of the promises of Christ.

Amen.

✠

Act of Contrition

O, my God, I am heartily sorry for having offended you. I detest all my sins because of your just punishment, but most of all because they offend you, my God, who are all-good and deserving of all my love. I firmly resolve, with the help of your grace, to sin no more and to avoid the near occasion of sin.

Amen.

✠

SHORT PRAYER
FOR MORNING

My God, I thank you for protecting me through the night. I praise you and give you thanks for all the blessings you have bestowed on me. In union with Jesus, I consecrate to you all my thoughts, words, actions, joys, and sufferings of this day. Mary, my mother, bless me this day and protect me from dangers. My Guardian Angel and all my patrons, pray for me.

Amen.

✠

PERSONAL PRAYER
FOR HEALING

Lord Jesus, I pray for your healing touch upon my body, mind, and spirit. I ask you to remove from me any fear or anxiety. Fill me with the peace that you alone can give. I place myself completely in your hands, Lord Jesus, trusting in your and love for me. May my recovery be swift, my strength renewed, and my health restored.

I place it all in your hands, Lord. You are the Divine Healer.

Amen.

✠

Prayer to
Saint Michael the Archangel

Saint Michael the Archangel, defend us in our day of battle; protect us against the deceit and wickedness of the devil. May God rebuke him, we humbly pray.

And you, O prince of the heavenly host, by the power of God banish into hell Satan and all of the evil spirits who roam through the world seeking the ruin of souls.

Amen.